Is it Quick?

Written by Monica Hughes

Is he quick?
Yes, he is quick.

Is it quick?
No, it is not quick.

The zebra has to be quick ...

... if his mum tells him to run.

Is he quick?
Yes, he is quick.

He can run and jump!

A heron has to be quick ...

... if he is to get a snack.

It has to be quick ...

... if a bug buzzes into its web.

I am quick …

... if my mum quacks at me.

I am not quick on land ...

... but I am quick if I swim!

Quick

Not quick